Awesome African Animals!

Giraffes Are Awesome!

by Lisa J. Amstutz

Consultant: Jackie Gai, DVM
Captive Wildlife Vet

raintree
a Capstone company — publishers for children

Raintree is an imprint of Capstone Global Library Limited, a company incorporated in England and Wales having its registered office at 7 Pilgrim Street, London, EC4V 6LB – Registered company number: 6695582

www.raintree.co.uk
myorders@raintree.co.uk

Edited by Mari Bolte and Erika Shores
Designed by Cynthia Della-Rovere
Picture research by Svetlana Zhurkin
Production by Morgan Walters
Printed and bound in China by Nordica.
0914/CA21401520

ISBN 978-1-406-28846-9
18 17 16 15 14
10 9 8 7 6 5 4 3 2 1

British Library Cataloguing in Publication Data
A full catalogue record for this book is available from the British Library.

Acknowledgements
Newscom: Photoshot/NHPA/Daryl Balfour, 24; Shutterstock: Achim Baque, 23, Black Sheep Media (grass), throughout, BlueRingMedia, 8 (right), Christian Musat, cover (bottom), 32, Coffeemill, cover (top left), 4 (left), 15 (right), Dennis Donohue, 6—7, Dmitry Pichugin, 26—27, fishandfish, 6 (left) and throughout (background), irakite, 12, jaroslava V, cover (right), 1, Jeff Grabert, 19, Jo Crebbin, 21, Joe McDonald, 18, Kletr, back cover (top), 26 (top), lewald, 9, Marci Paravia, 13, MattiaATH, 20, Mogens Trolle, 11, Mohamed Zain, 15 (left), moizhusein, 29, mythja, 10 (top right), Nadezhda Bolotina, 22, orxy, 25, Pal Teravagimov, 28, Pyty, 4—5, Shinga, 17, spirit of America (African landscape), back cover and throughout, stieberszabolcs, 4 (middle), studio online, 14, Tzido Sun, 8 (left), Vaclav Volrab, 10 (left, bottom)

We would like to thank Jackie Gai, DVM, for her invaluable help in the preparation of this book.

Every effort has been made to contact copyright holders of material reproduced in this book. Any omissions will be rectified in subsequent printings if notice is given to the publisher.

Contents

All about giraffes

Stretch! A giraffe reaches high up into a tree. It nibbles a tasty leaf. Giraffes are the tallest land animals. They grow up to 5.5 metres (18 feet) tall.

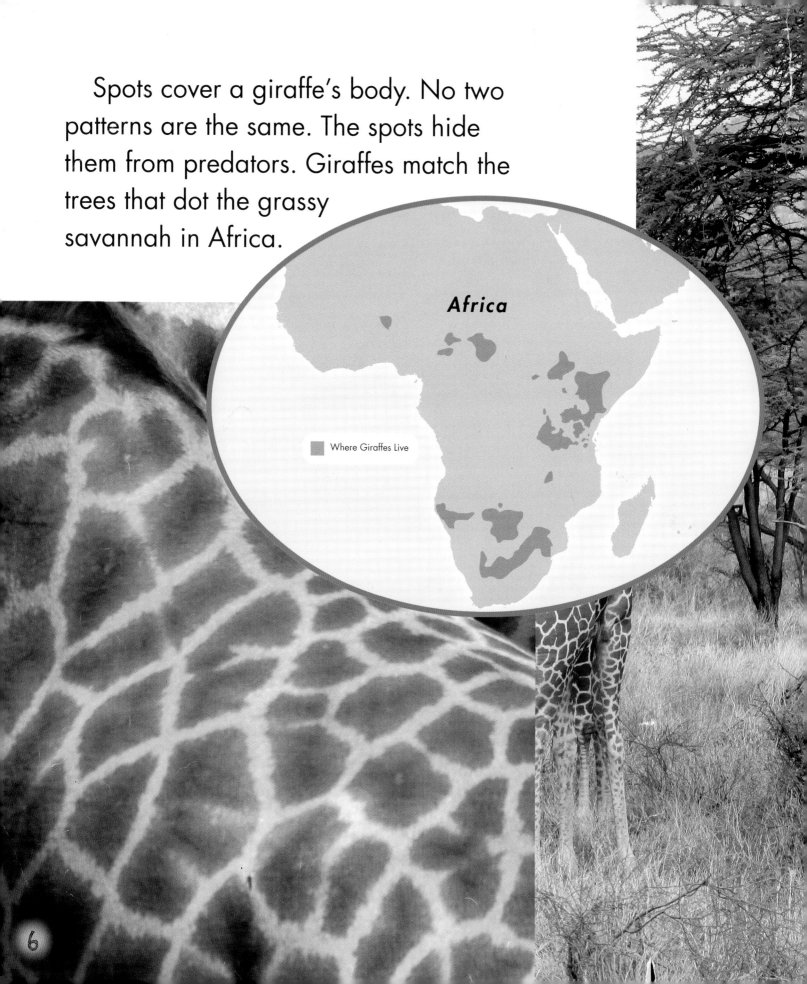

Spots cover a giraffe's body. No two patterns are the same. The spots hide them from predators. Giraffes match the trees that dot the grassy savannah in Africa.

Africa

Where Giraffes Live

A giraffe's neck is as long as its legs. Short hair, called a mane, grows down the neck. Inside the neck are seven bones. Your neck has seven bones, too. They are much smaller than a giraffe's, though!

A giraffee's long neck makes it hard to jump up quickly from lying down. So giraffes often sleep standing up.

The bumps on a giraffe's head are called ossicones. They are made of bone, and are covered with skin and hair. Males, called bulls, use them to fight each other. They crash their heads and necks together. They fight over females, called cows.

Dinner time

Giraffes are herbivores. That means they eat only plants. It takes lots of food to fill a giraffe's stomach. It can eat 34 kilograms (75 pounds) of food in one day. A giraffe eats in the morning and evening. It rests in the heat of the day and at night.

Giraffes eat leaves, twigs and small branches. They grab food from the tops of trees with their long tongues. A giraffe's tongue is as long as your arm!

Giraffes love eating from acacia trees. The tree has sharp thorns. But the giraffe's tongue and gums are tough. Its strong teeth crush the thorns. Thick saliva protects its mouth.

A giraffe's stomach has four parts. The food goes into the first part. Then the giraffe burps it up and chews it again. Now it is called cud. After a while, the giraffe swallows the cud. It then passes through the rest of the giraffe's stomach.

Family Ties

At the age of 5, a female giraffe can have a calf. A newborn calf is 1.8 metres (6 feet) tall. It starts walking soon after birth. The calf drinks its mother's milk at first. Later it will learn to eat leaves.

For its first week, a calf hides in tall grass. Its mother stays near by. Then it joins other calves in the herd. Their mothers take turns watching them. Living in a herd keeps calves safe. Once fully grown, giraffes in the wild can live to 25 years old.

Danger lurks

A giraffe can drink 38 litres (10 gallons) of water at a time. It can go days without drinking. When it drinks, the giraffe spreads its legs and bends down. During this time, predators can attack.

Giraffes go to watering holes in groups. They take turns watching for predators. They warn the others with grunts and snorts when danger is near.

Adult giraffes are too big for most predators to kill. But they have to watch out for lions and crocodiles. Hyenas and cheetahs can kill calves.

Giraffes have good eyesight and hearing. Their height lets them spot predators far away. So zebras and other animals like to graze near them.

When a predator comes near, giraffes run away. They can run up to 56 kilometres (35 miles) per hour for short distances. They can kick hard, too. A powerful kick can kill a lion.

Saving giraffes

Humans are the biggest danger to giraffes. People hunt them for their meat and skins. Farmers cut down the trees giraffes eat, to grow crops and raise livestock.

Today most giraffes live in wildlife parks and reserves. There they are safe from hunters. People plant trees for them. If we protect giraffes, these awesome giants will always roam Africa.

Glossary

cud half-eaten food that an animal burps up and chews again

graze eat grass and other plants

herbivore animal that eats only plants

herd large group of animals that live or move together

mane long, thick hair that grows on the head and neck of some animals such as lions and horses

ossicone bump on a giraffe's head

predator animal that hunts other animals for food

reserve area of land set aside by the government for a special purpose such as protecting plants and animals

saliva clear liquid in the mouth

savannah flat, grassy area of land with few or no trees

Books

Laughing Giraffe (African Animal Tales), Mwenye Hadithi (Hodder Children's Books, 2009)

DK First Animal Encyclopedia (DK First Reference Series), Penelope Arlon (Dorling Kindersley, 2004)

Websites

www.cotswoldwildlifepark.co.uk/meet-animals/giraffe.htm
Meet the giraffes, and find out more about this amazing African animal!

http://kids.nationalgeographic.com/content/kids/en_US/ animals/giraffe/
Does a giraffe weigh more than a piano? Find this answer and more!

Comprehension questions

1. Why might a giraffe's long neck make it difficult for it to get up quickly?

2. Describe how a giraffe's tongue helps it to eat.

3. The text on page 10 says male giraffes use their ossicones for fighting. What do you think females use their ossicones for?

Index